Contents

Secret Tunnels

by
David Orme

Ransom

Thunderbolts

Secret Tunnels
by David Orme

Illustrated by Dylan Gibson

Published by Ransom Publishing Ltd.
Radley House, 8 St. Cross Road, Winchester, Hants. SO23 9HX, UK
www.ransom.co.uk

ISBN   978 178127 072 1

First published in 2013

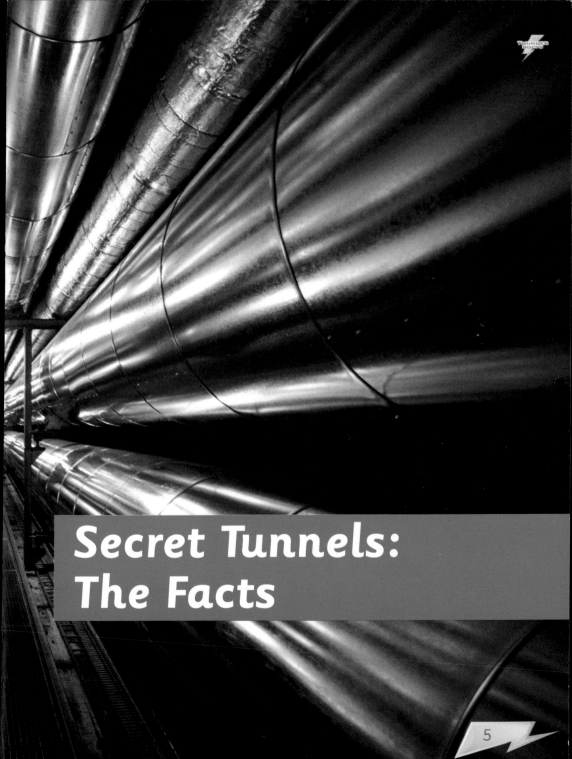

Secret Tunnels:
The Facts

Pyramid tunnels

The Great Pyramid in Egypt.

Inside the Great Pyramid.

The King's chamber

tunnels

Inside the Great Pyramid.

The King's chamber.

Catacombs are tunnels for dead bodies.

8

Palermo, Italy

Poland

London, U.K.

9

Cave paintings

These paintings were made 17,000 years ago!

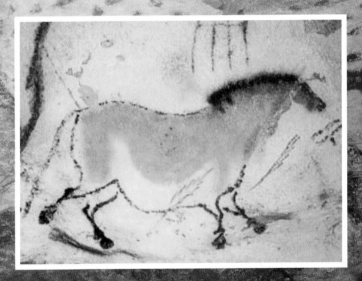

They weren't found until 1940.

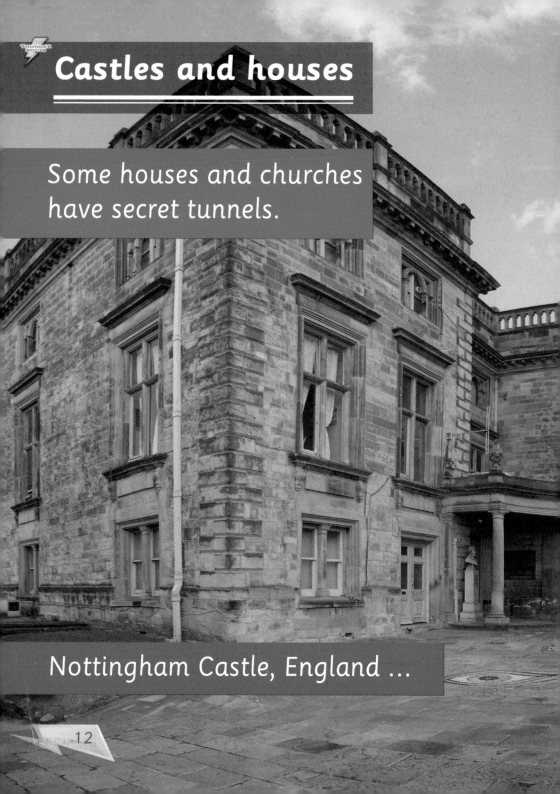

Castles and houses

Some houses and churches have secret tunnels.

Nottingham Castle, England ...

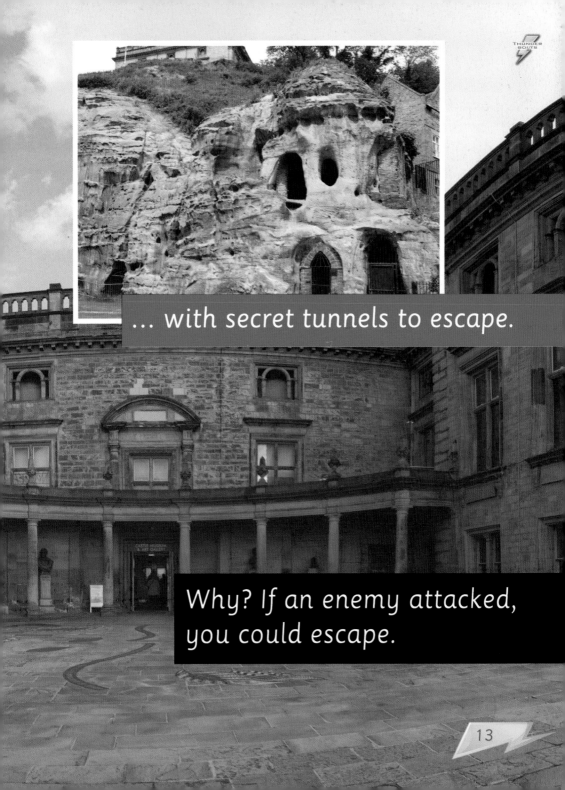

... with secret tunnels to escape.

Why? If an enemy attacked, you could escape.

How to hide your tunnel

This is the entrance
to a secret room!

A secret trap door.

A secret entrance to underground tunnels.

15

Underground cities

An old underground city in Turkey.

20,000 people could live here.

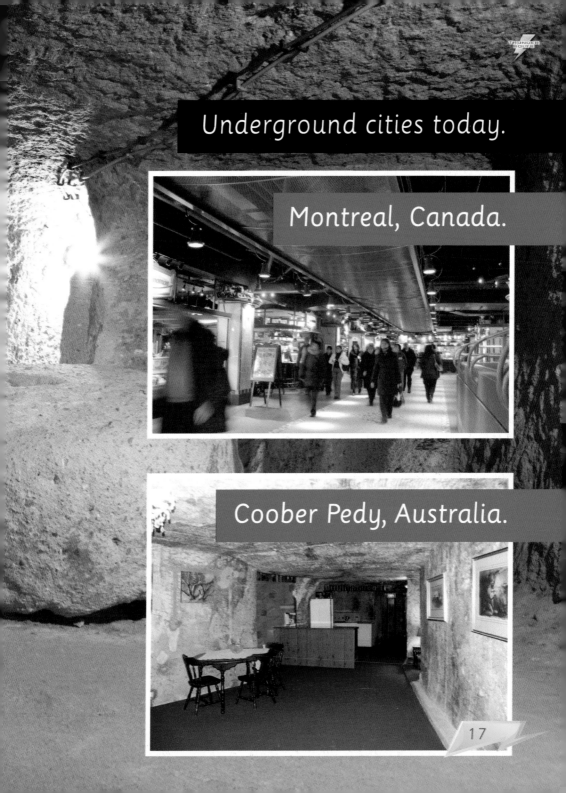

Underground cities today.

Montreal, Canada.

Coober Pedy, Australia.

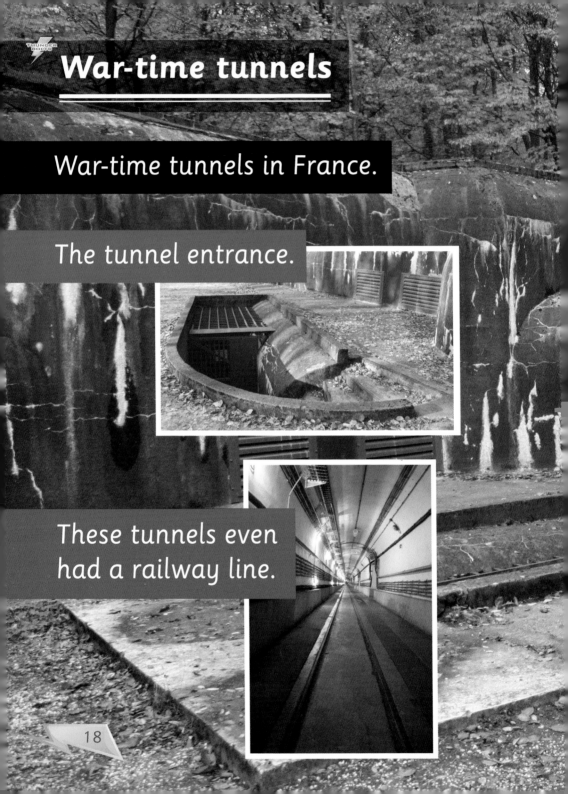

War-time tunnels

War-time tunnels in France.

The tunnel entrance.

These tunnels even had a railway line.

An underground hospital.

19

Keeping safe in war-time

People sheltering in an underground station in London.

Bed-time!

Russian children take shelter during an air raid.

Secret bunkers

A bunker defends people from attack.

The entrance to a secret nuclear bunker!

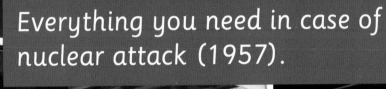

Everything you need in case of nuclear attack (1957).

FALLOUT SHELTER ↑ 5 MI

Treasure Maze

It's a really bad storm ...

The tunnel went on and on ...

Wow, treasure!

We're rich!

29

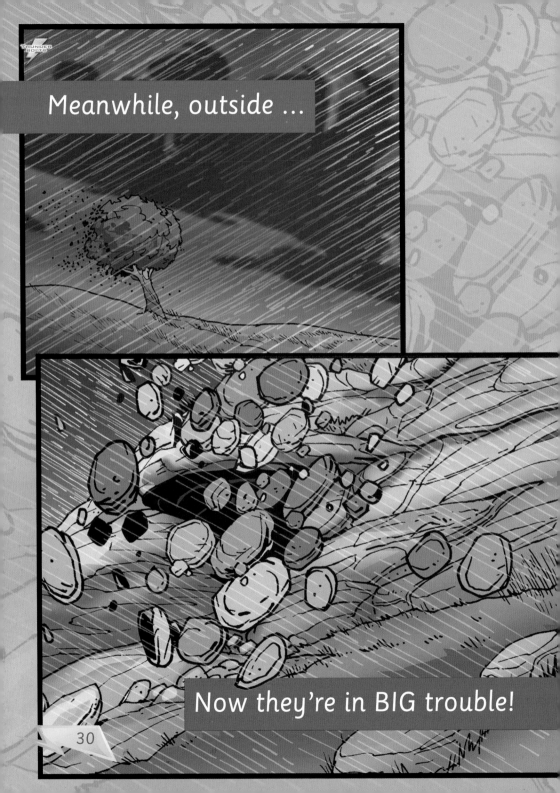

Meanwhile, outside ...

Now they're in BIG trouble!

Maybe there's another way out.

Let's try this one.

Bad idea!

Last chance!

This is our last chance!

Are they doomed? Maybe not!

Will they make it?

Where on Earth are they?

Help!

Just above their heads ...

Help!

Safe at last!

Word list

Australia	hospital
bunker	nuclear
Canada	painting
castle	Poland
catacombs	pyramid
chamber	shelter
enemy	treasure
entrance	Turkey
escape	underground